Abandoned Upon Arrival, Implications for Refugees and Local Communities Burdened by a U.S. Resettlement System that is Not Working: July 21, 2010

U.S. Government Printing Office

The BiblioGov Project is an effort to expand awareness of the public documents and records of the U.S. Government via print publications. In broadening the public understanding of government and its work, an enlightened democracy can grow and prosper. Ranging from historic Congressional Bills to the most recent Budget of the United States Government, the BiblioGov Project spans a wealth of government information. These works are now made available through an environmentally friendly, print-on-demand basis, using only what is necessary to meet the required demands of an interested public. We invite you to learn of the records of the U.S. Government, heightening the knowledge and debate that can lead from such publications.

Included are the following Collections:

Budget of The United States Government	Code of Federal Regulations
Presidential Documents	Congressional Documents
United States Code	Economic Indicators
Education Reports from ERIC	Federal Register
GAO Reports	Government Manuals
History of Bills	House Journal
House Rules and Manual	Privacy act Issuances
Public and Private Laws	Statutes at Large

111TH CONGRESS 2d Session	COMMITTEE PRINT	S. PRT. 111–52

ABANDONED UPON ARRIVAL: IMPLICATIONS FOR REFUGEES AND LOCAL COMMUNITIES BURDENED BY A U.S. RESETTLEMENT SYSTEM THAT IS NOT WORKING

A REPORT

TO THE MEMBERS

OF THE

COMMITTEE ON FOREIGN RELATIONS

UNITED STATES SENATE

ONE HUNDRED ELEVENTH CONGRESS
SECOND SESSION

JULY 21, 2010

Printed for the use of the Committee on Foreign Relations

Available via World Wide Web:
http://www.gpoaccess.gov/congress/index.html

U.S. GOVERNMENT PRINTING OFFICE
WASHINGTON : 2010

57–483 PDF

For sale by the Superintendent of Documents, U.S. Government Printing Office
Internet: bookstore.gpo.gov   Phone: toll free (866) 512–1800; DC area (202) 512–1800
Fax: (202) 512–2104   Mail: Stop IDCC, Washington, DC 20402–0001

COMMITTEE ON FOREIGN RELATIONS

JOHN F. KERRY, Massachusetts, *Chairman*

CHRISTOPHER J. DODD, Connecticut
RUSSELL D. FEINGOLD, Wisconsin
BARBARA BOXER, California
ROBERT MENENDEZ, New Jersey
BENJAMIN L. CARDIN, Maryland
ROBERT P. CASEY, JR., Pennsylvania
JIM WEBB, Virginia
JEANNE SHAHEEN, New Hampshire
EDWARD E. KAUFMAN, Delaware
KIRSTEN E. GILLIBRAND, New York

RICHARD G. LUGAR, Indiana
BOB CORKER, Tennessee
JOHNNY ISAKSON, Georgia
JAMES E. RISCH, Idaho
JIM DeMINT, South Carolina
JOHN BARRASSO, Wyoming
ROGER F. WICKER, Mississippi
JAMES M. INHOFE, Oklahoma

FRANK G. LOWENSTEIN, *Staff Director*
KENNETH A. MYERS, JR., *Republican Staff Director*

CONTENTS

	Page
Letter of Transmittal	v
Introduction	1
Findings	2
Recommendations	4
Overview	6
Case Study: Fort Wayne, Indiana	7
Case Study: Clarkston, Georgia	11
Conclusion	14
Acknowledgements	15
Appendix I—Summary of Refugee Admissions as of 30 April, 2010	17
Appendix II—Official Letter from City of Fort Wayne, Indiana	19
Appendix III—Refugee Article in the News-Sentinel	21
Appendix IV—Refugee Article in the Journal Gazette	23
Appendix V—Refugee Article in the New York Times	24
Appendix VI—Legislation Introduced in the Georgia General Assembly, April 2003	37
Appendix VII—Acronyms	38

(III)

LETTER OF TRANSMITTAL

United States Senate,
Committee on Foreign Relations,
Washington, DC, July 21, 2010.

Dear Colleagues: Since 1975, the United States has offered safe-haven to nearly 3 million refugees who faced persecution in Communist-controlled and conflict-ridden regions of the world. This resettlement reflects our Nation's noblest humanitarian traditions, and should continue. But we must acknowledge that significant costs are associated with this activity.

After consulting with community stakeholders in Indiana and elsewhere, and in light of the recent Presidential directive authorizing the admission of up to 80,000 refugees in FY 2010, I asked the Foreign Relations Committee minority staff, who have long monitored the conditions of vulnerable refugee populations during their travels, under the leadership of professional staff member Garrett Johnson to assess the government's policies and programs for refugee admission and resettlement. Staff found that resettlement efforts in some U.S. cities are underfunded, overstretched, and failing to meet the basic needs of the refugee populations they are currently asked to assist. Especially in a difficult economic climate, the current structure of the U.S. resettlement system is proving a strain on local resources and community relations.

As a former mayor, I am sensitive to the challenges faced by resettlement cities in Indiana and across the country. U.S. refugee policies and procedures are determined at the Federal level, but the burdens of addressing the unique needs of refugees after they arrive are passed on to local communities, often without their consent. Some resettled refugees are illiterate in their native language or suffer from severe physical or mental ailments and many are ill-equipped to secure employment in an increasingly competitive job market. The financial and mentoring assistance required to help this population achieve self-sufficiency exceeds the resources currently provided by the Federal Government.

In Fort Wayne, IN, educators working with large refugee populations resettled in the city have expressed frustration because they lack the time and tools to address the extraordinary needs of refugee students. Poor performances on mandated standardized tests by some recently arrived refugee students, who often lack basic education after languishing in refugee camps for a decade or more, are negatively impacting the overall scores and reputations of schools. Public health officials also have raised concerns that some refugee populations, who have been found to suffer from elevated rates of latent tuberculosis (TB), are not undergoing adequate prearrival screening or properly monitoring their own treatment. Consequently, they face a higher risk of developing active TB, which is contagious and a potential health threat to the general population.

The administration must demonstrate clearly to Congress and resettlement communities how federal resources will be better matched with refugee admissions. In order to supplement this report and the administration's inquiry, I have also asked the Government Accountability Office to undertake a comprehensive review of the U.S. refugee resettlement system. In the future, the administration may determine that an increase in Federal funding or decrease in refugee admissions is warranted. But the practice of passing the costs of resettling refugees on to local communities should not continue.

I was pleased to learn recently that Representative Anh "Joseph" Cao of Louisiana, who fled Communist-controlled Vietnam in 1975 as a refugee, was sponsored by a family from Goshen, IN, and spent many of his formative years as a Hoosier. His success and service as the first Vietnamese-American Member of Congress exemplifies the potential benefits gained by our country through offering safe haven to the persecuted of the world. The administration and Congress must ensure that the refugee resettlement system is properly structured so that it continues to be perceived as a benefit and not a burden.

This report and its recommendations are particularly timely given that discussions on reforming the refugee resettlement system have been initiated within the administration. I look forward to continuing to work with you on these issues, and I welcome any comments you have.

Sincerely,

RICHARD G. LUGAR,
Ranking Member.

ABANDONED UPON ARRIVAL: IMPLICATIONS FOR REFUGEES AND LOCAL COMMUNITIES BURDENED BY A U.S. RESETTLEMENT SYSTEM THAT IS NOT WORKING

INTRODUCTION

The United States, historically, is a nation of immigrants. In recent decades, however, it has also become a nation of refugees. Since 1975, the year in which hundreds of thousands of persons from Communist-controlled Vietnam started arriving on our shores, the United States has officially accepted for resettlement roughly 2.9 million refugees from strife-torn countries around the world. The United States has resettled more refugees than any other country.

Legally, a refugee is someone admitted to the United States after Federal agencies have made a determination that he or she has been persecuted or has well-founded fear of potential persecution based on race, nationality, religion, membership in a particular group or political opinion and is unable or unwilling to return to their country of origin. By contrast, the majority of immigrants allowed to enter America generally decide to relocate for family reunion or economic reasons.

But experience has shown that there are also important qualitative differences between the two groups. Some refugee populations currently arriving in the United States have languished in refugee camps for nearly a decade or more. They are reported to have a much greater need for prolonged government support if they are to become conversant, employed and self-sufficient. Some are illiterate in their native language, these refugees have limited formal education, suffer from serious health or psychological conditions and lack the basic skills required to compete in an increasingly strained job market.

In order to better understand the challenges confronting resettlement cities and the refugees admitted to the United States, Senator Richard Lugar, ranking member of the Senate Foreign Relations Committee, asked staff to assess the government's policies and programs for refugee admissions and resettlement. This study finds that resettlement efforts in many U.S. cities are underfunded, overstretched, and failing to meet the basic needs of the refugee populations they are currently asked to assist. Especially in a difficult economic climate, the study recommends that the Federal Government do more to support and resource the local communities who bear the responsibilities of receiving this increased flow. This study concludes that the policies promulgated in the Refugee Act of 1980 and the current system of refugee processing, orientation, placement, and resettlement assistance are out-dated and fail to address the needs of the culturally and linguistically diverse populations now being admitted to the United States.

This report will attempt to underscore a number of critical challenges confronting the refugee resettlement system and offer recommendations for better supporting local resettlement communities as well as improving the quality of assistance offered to refugees admitted to the United States.

FINDINGS

1. Under current practice, the Federal Government works with national voluntary organizations, including faith-based groups, to decide on where to send refugees for resettlement. These newcomers place demands, sometimes significant, on local schools, police, hospitals and social services. Local governments are often burdened with the weight of addressing the unique assistance refugees require, yet they rarely have an official role in influencing how many refugees are resettled by local voluntary agencies and often are not even informed in advance that new residents will be arriving.

2. Although the ability to communicate—even on a basic level—is essential to the survival of refugee populations (e.g., access to employment for adults and educational opportunities for youth), resources for language instruction are inadequate. Unlike migrants in search of economic opportunities, who can often access extensive friend and family networks to navigate language or other cultural barriers, new refugee populations lack this type of community resource upon arrival. The language barrier often impedes the ability of refugees to navigate local health care systems with a potential wide impact on the general public health. Interviews conducted for this study with law enforcement officials also revealed grave public safety concerns, as language barriers often limit the ability of officers to communicate with refugees during emergency situations.

A 2009 study completed by the Georgetown Law Human Rights Institute, based on consultations with Iraqi refugee communities in Washington, DC, Detroit, San Diego, and the country of Jordan, found that "refugees have difficulty accessing English language training, the quality of instruction is poor, and there are simply not enough classes available for all refugees."[1] A 2008 study commissioned by the Office of Refugee Resettlement within the U.S. Department of Health and Human Services clearly noted that refugees arriving with some level of English proficiency, as well as those who receive ESL services, often have better outcomes.[2]

3. At present, efforts to address the special needs of refugee students are ad hoc, a drain on local education funding, and implemented in the absence of data-driven best practices. Within the cities examined for this report, several schools labeled as failing or facing imminent risk of being taken over by state authorities have a high refugee student population. School administrators complained that refugee students—sometimes within weeks of arriving in the United States—are required to take standardized tests and

---

[1] Adess, S. et al. (2009). "Refugee Crisis in America: Iraqis and Their Resettlement Experience." Washington, DC: Georgetown Law, available at www.law.georgetown.edu/news/.../RefugeeCrisisinAmerica_000.pdf.

[2] Farrell, M. et al. (2008). "The Evaluation of the Refugee Social Services (RSS) and Targeted Assistance Formula Grant (TAG) Programs: Synthesis of Findings From Three Sites." (Prepared by the Lewin Group and commissioned by the U.S. Department of Health and Human Services.) Available at www.lewin.com/content/publications/3871.pdf.

their often poor performance is detrimental to the school's overall score. School administrators also reported receiving little to no additional Federal or State resources to increase staffing levels and offer additional assistance addressing the psycho-social-cultural needs of refugee students.

4. Currently, irrespective of important factors such as education level, health condition or psychological background each refugee is initially afforded one-size-fits-all assistance. Further, resettlement locations are provided very little, if any, prearrival information regarding these important factors, which could help the city to better prepare its social service infrastructure in anticipation of increased demands. For example, in Fort Wayne, IN, a pattern of elevated rates of hepatitis B among the Burmese was simply "stumbled upon" by local public health officials. The costly treatment associated with this life-long condition presents another significant cost the local community will be forced to bear.

Unfortunately, federal funding formulas used to forecast resources provided to resettlement cities have proven too inflexible and backward-looking to respond to such public health concerns. The issue of monitoring when and where refugees move after they are initially resettled in the United States, known as secondary migration, also presents a critical challenge to the backward-looking funding system. Secondary migration within the first 8 months of resettlement can create hidden populations of unsupported refugees. There is currently no system in place to transfer refugee entitlement benefits (e.g., medical insurance, housing support, welfare support) from State to State, placing a further unexpected strain on communities.

5. The initial per capita grant awarded directly to refugees for the first 30–90 days after arrival was increased from roughly $450 to $1,100 in January 2010.[3] Prior to this increase, refugees were essentially consigned to poverty upon entering the United States, as the decades-old grant level had declined by more than 50 percent in real terms due to inflation. However, this increase, although welcomed, is proving to only delay the incidence of poverty, as many refugees lack a legitimate shot at becoming employed, conversant, and self-sufficient under the current system.

6. There is limited Federal funding available to support programs that assist refugees after the initial resettlement assistance expires. Resources that exist are often not widely advertised, difficult to access and no technical assistance is made available to help local communities with submitting grant applications.

7. From the perspective of local resettlement cities, it is clear that the Federal Government has failed to communicate what actions, if any, are being taken to build a resettlement system capable of accommodating the refugees authorized by the presidential directive for FY 2010, without placing additional strain on local community resources and detracting from the services extended to current refugees in-country.

---

[3] In January, PRM increased the total Reception and Placement grant from $900 to $1,800. Of this amount, the local resettlement agency can use up to $700 to cover administrative expenses (i.e., salaries, rent, utilities, supplies, etc.). The remaining $1,100 must be spent on behalf of refugees. On a pilot basis, PRM gave local resettlement agencies some spending flexibility—requiring at least $900 to be spent on each refugee and the balance of $200 may be spent on other cases requiring additional financial assistance.

RECOMMENDATIONS

1. *Enhance Formal Consultations with State and Local Leaders:* The Bureau of Population Refugees and Migration (PRM) within the Department of State should restructure the process by which refugee resettlement is determined to include formal participation and consent from local leaders. Currently, voluntary agencies funded to provide placement services are only required by PRM to, in writing, briefly:

> Describe the date, content, and results of consultative discussions undertaken by the affiliate with state and local officials in preparing this proposal, including the response of the state refugee coordinator. For new sites, include evidence of consultations with and support of other local affiliates, refugee and community service providers, and the state refugee coordinator.[4]

The restructured process should require local resettlement agencies to formally consult with state and local officials/service providers in the resettlement site area regarding the proposed number and backgrounds of refugees to be resettled in the area. The qualitative and quantitative input given by local communities should be included as part of the Refugee Funding Proposals (RFPs) submitted by resettlement agencies.

The refugee coordinators in each state and PRM representatives should verify that the consultations took place and that the views of the officials/service providers are accurately characterized in the RFPs. In cases of irreconcilable opinions amongst key stakeholders regarding absorptive capacity, the state refugee coordinator should be able to request a moratorium for the community. During this deferral period, PRM should engage community leaders and voluntary agencies in order to achieve consensus. The moratorium would make exception for cases of immediate family reunification.

2. *Improve Access to English as Second Language (ESL) Courses:* The administration should consider strategies, informed by best practices, for providing prearrival language instruction and enhanced access to longer term ESL classes once resettled so that more refugees are placed on a path to proficiency and eventual self-sufficiency. Among the top priorities of such strategies, as suggested by experts consulted for this report, should be allocating funding specifically for refugee language training and exploring ways to make some public assistance offered to refugees conditional upon ESL class attendance to incentivize proficiency. Courses should meet basic qualification standards in order to ensure quality control.

3. *Invest in Education:* The administration should formulate national strategies, consistent with best practices, for engaging schools that are tasked with meeting the unique psycho-social-cultural needs of refugee students, so as not to detract from the quality of instruction offered to the general student population. Among

---

[4] PRM Official Document obtained in April 2010, "FY 2010 Affiliate/Sub-Office Abstract."

the top priorities of such strategies, as suggested by educators consulted for this report [5], should be efforts which:

A. Create a "new-comers" program that delays the immersion of some refugee youth into the general student population and provides them, in a separated environment, instructors and curricula informed by best practices. Implemented with Federal funding, the program would evaluate each refugee's educational, psychological, and physiological status as well as provide intensive academic, cultural, and English language instruction.

B. Grant waivers to some refugee youth, under conditions determined by a panel of experts, exempting their scores on mandated standardized tests from negatively influencing overall school performance due to the often extraordinary circumstances surrounding their initial resettlement.

C. Increase funding and support for adult educational and vocational training as well as recertification programs for nontraditional refugee students. Encourage ESL training that is linked to prevocational education in order to facilitate learning for employment.

4. *Discard One-Size-Fits-All Approach:* The overall resettlement system must be structured to identify and address the diverse needs of resettling populations. This should involve overseas gathering of information that is used to help local communities plan for and better meet refugee needs. Both the United Nations High Commissioner for Refugees (UNHCR) and Overseas Processing Entities (OPE) currently interview refugees and asylum—seekers numerous times and at length throughout the adjudication process and before admission. Additional information could be collected either at the level of OPE processing and/or to be completed by UNHCR when completing the resettlement referral form. ORR, state refugee coordinators, local officials and voluntary agencies should be consulted in determining what type of information would be helpful to improving local service delivery and capacity planning. Additionally, this information should inform broad strategic planning before processing and placement begins.

The administration should also ensure that funding formulas used to forecast resources provided to resettlement cities are more flexible, forward-looking and responsive to secondary migration flows.

5. *Improve Accountability:* The administration should examine:

A. Institutional processes and practices of voluntary agencies, including but not limited to factors that influence the scope of an agency's annual refugee resettlement proposal submitted to PRM, organizational structure, and administrative overhead to ensure an adherence to best practices and a resettlement program that is sensitive to local community capacity.

B. Oversight and accountability metrics used by PRM for monitoring voluntary agencies as well as mechanisms for assessing internal strengths and inefficiencies within PRM's administrative processes, the nature of PRM's consultations with

---

[5] The recommendations reflect the opinions of educators from East Allen Community Schools and Fort Wayne Community Schools.

local and state elected officials, and the factors influencing the annual cap of refugees admitted to the United States.

C. Mechanisms used for assessing internal strengths and inefficiencies in the Office of Refugee Resettlement (ORR) within the Department of Health and Human Services, the nature of ORR's consultations with local and state elected officials, and the extent of ORR's capacity to oversee voluntary agency grantees, address the unique needs of refugees, fact-find into community capacity shortfalls as well as monitor the impact of secondary migration—potentially through some type of targeted census.

D. Metrics for evaluating refugee integration, including but not limited to qualitative and quantitative measurements of employment levels, language acquisition, community interaction, etc.

E. Interagency coordination, including information-sharing and planning-coordination between ORR and PRM as well as the potential value added by establishing a centralized position to coordinate long- and short-term refugee policy housed within or reportable to the White House.

6. *Explore Innovative Models:* The administration should engage State and local leaders with experience and expertise advancing local solutions to the challenges currently under review at the Federal level. The development and implementation of innovative resettlement models that incorporate lessons learned informed by grassroots experimentation should be encouraged and resourced.

7. *Promote Community Engagement:* The administration should require voluntary agencies to submit as part of their annual proposals a "community engagement strategy," which delineates concrete plans for increasing public awareness of and interaction with refugees, in order to achieve greater community cohesion. Unfortunately, the onus of initiating and funding this type of intercultural awareness and engagement is often left to individuals and community organizations and is usually ad hoc at best.

Providing opportunities for established residents and families to engage members of the refugee population will help to demystify preconceptions and make integration more achievable. Encouraging face-to-face interactions between individuals or small groups can also make inter-ethnic encounters less intimidating for all participants.

OVERVIEW

The United States has welcomed nearly 3 million refugees to this country since the 1970s, demonstrating our Nation's commitment to protecting those who face persecution throughout the world.[6] But what becomes of the refugees and the locations in which they settle after they arrive?

A 2009 study conducted by Georgetown Law Human Rights Institute, based on consultation with Iraqi refugee communities in Washington, DC, Detroit, San Diego, and the country of Jordan, offered the following findings:

---
[6] See appendix I. "PRM Office of Admission—Refugee Processing Center, Summary of Refugee Admissions as of 30 April 2010."

The United States is opening its gates to refugees and simply forgetting about them after they have arrived. In the process, the United States is in danger of failing to meet its legal obligations to extend protection to the most vulnerable refugees, promote their long-term self-sufficiency, and support their integration. . . .

Employment services, provided by [voluntary agencies] and State agencies, are seriously underfunded and unable to adequately help Iraqi refugees in their job search. Lack of transportation remains a significant barrier to securing and maintaining employment. English as a Second Language (ESL) classes, generally inadequate in both quality and duration, fail to help Iraqis build marketable language skills. In addition, the opportunity to pursue education and recertification programs, prerequisites for many jobs, is either unavailable or eclipsed by more immediate needs. Given these barriers, it is not surprising that the vast majority of Iraqi refugees interviewed were unemployed despite expressing a strong desire to work.[7]

Field research undertaken for this study in the cities of Fort Wayne, Indiana, and Clarkston, Georgia, made similar findings.[8] The challenges confronting the U.S. refugee assistance program, much like those confronting our nation's immigration policies in general, are significant and systemic. Strong leadership by the administration and Congress will be needed to offer a clear and practical way forward.

Case Study: Fort Wayne, IN

After nearly two decades of welcoming and resettling refugees from disparate regions of the world the city of Fort Wayne, with a population of roughly 300,000, determined that it had reached a breaking point. City officials and community stakeholders felt they were sustaining a broken system on limited community resources and a wealth of goodwill. The city in November 2008 officially requested a resettlement moratorium from the State Family Social Services Administration.[9] The city has accepted thousands of refugees throughout the years, starting with persons from South East Asia in 1975, but complained that the confluence of a tough economic climate and inadequate federal resources caused the latest influx of refugees to become unbearable.

The State of Indiana responded by stopping new arrivals to the city, except in the case of family reunification. But the problems caused by the existing refugee population and the post-arrival relocation of refugees, known as secondary migration, remain a concern. The city has appealed to Federal authorities for assistance, so far to little avail. A once-welcoming environment has become what some persons interviewed called a "potentially explosive situation." They cite recent examples in the local press of confronta-

---

[7] Adess, S. et al. (2009). "Refugee Crisis in America: Iraqis and Their Resettlement Experience." Washington, DC: Georgetown Law Human Rights Institute. Available at www.law.georgetown.edu/news/.../RefugeeCrisisinAmerica_000.pdf.

[8] The interviews and field visits that contribute to this study were conducted over the course of several years—from 2008 to present—and may have been used in other documents generated by the author.

[9] See appendix II. Official letter from Office of the Mayor, city of Fort Wayne, IN.

tions between American citizens and refugees. The most recent incident allegedly involved Burmese refugees publicly relieving themselves and/or spitting betel nut juice in a local laundromat store, which resulted in an employee of this business placing a sign on the door stating "For sanitary reasons, there are no Burmese people allowed." [10]

The historical flows of refugee resettlements in Fort Wayne are estimated by local officials to originally have been between 100 and 200 each year. This was considered manageable, even if underresourced, by most within the community. Fred Gilbert, a community advocate for refugees, noted that most citizens were oblivious to the refugee population and were unaware that the resettlement program existed. However, decisions made at the Federal level to admit a higher number of Burmese refugees to the United States, many of whom had languished in refugee camps for nearly a decade or more, resulted in a dramatic and unexpected increase in refugees arriving in Fort Wayne in 2007.

According to elected officials and community leaders, the city received roughly 700 Burmese refugees in 2007 and 800 in 2008 without any notice of their impending arrival. Moreover, numerous city officials interviewed for this study said they had never been asked by resettlement agencies or by PRM whether the city could handle the newcomers.

Coinciding with this increase in refugees was the global economic recession and decrease in demand for low-skilled labor throughout the region. For example, Elkhart, IN, visited by President Obama in February 2009 to underscore the Nation's depressed job markets, is roughly a 1.5 hour drive from Fort Wayne. It had an unemployment rate in March 2010 of 15.2 percent, compared to Ft. Wayne's 11.1 percent.

While the pace of resettlement dropped due to restrictions limiting new placements to family reunification, Fort Wayne has emerged as a "community of choice" for many Burmese resettled elsewhere around the country. Although no official system for tracking so-called secondary migration currently exists, city leaders estimate that Burmese have arrived at a rate of two secondary migrants for each refugee directly resettled in the city. The resources required to assist this flow of secondary migrants are not being directed to Fort Wayne because ORR and PRM have not established a mechanism for tracking such migration patterns. The significant strain accompanying secondary migrants was identified by each interviewee as Fort-Wayne's most pressing refugee-related challenge.

The concern surrounding secondary migration is warranted because some refugee populations have proven to pose special resettlement challenges. Many of the more than 6,000 Burmese refugees in Fort Wayne are illiterate in their native language, have few marketable skills, and are accustomed to government dependence after being confined to refugee camps for a decade or more. The de-

---

[10] See appendix III and IV. Kevin Leininger. "'No Burmese' Sign Draws Ire: Despite Business Owners Apology, City's Civil Rights Watchdog Is Investigating." News-Sentinel, 10 March 2010. Available at http://www.news-sentinel.com/apps/pbcs.dll/article?AID=/20100310/NEWS/3100340. Devon Haynie. "Burmese Demand Action on Prejudice: See Official Indifference to Sign at Laundry." Journal Gazette, 15 March 2010. Available at http://www.journalgazette.net/article/20100315/LOCAL/303159989.

mand that they become conversant, employed, and self-sufficient within PRM's 90-day time limit was deemed "cruel and unethical" by Dr. Jeanne Zehr, assistant superintendent of East Allen Community Schools.

Dr. Zehr noted that the five schools in her system with the highest population of refugee youth are considered to have the lowest academic performance rates according to Indiana accountability standards.[11] She argued that many refugee youth should not be expected to compete with their American peers when they have "never even seen a toilet or flushed a toilet because they were born in those camps." An American parent at one of the failing elementary schools, Dr. Zehr said, tried to lead an effort to have other parents withdraw their American students because she felt that the refugee youth were detrimental to her child's educational experience. The parents' appeal did not gain traction, but this type of response appears symptomatic of a general frustration.

The superintendent of Fort Wayne Community Schools, Dr. Wendy Robinson, acknowledged that two schools in her system with large refugee populations face imminent risk of being taken over by State authorities because of chronic underperformance.[12] Dr. Robinson stated, "We are robbing Peter to pay Paul. . . . The one-size-fits-all approach is just not working." The reality on the ground is that money is regularly diverted from other programs to address the special needs of refugee youth because "they're our kids once they are here," she said.

In FY 2009, East Allen Community Schools received $21,000 and $15,000 went to Fort Wayne Community Schools as part of a larger $150,000 School Impact grant awarded to Indiana by ORR, but such a small grant is considered to be insufficient. Dr. Robinson contended, "I need nurses, translators, psychologists. I visited one of my schools on the first day of the year and not one of the [refugee] students or parents spoke English. $15,000 is just a drop in the bucket."

Emphasis was placed on the need for additional staffing to address the unique backgrounds of refugee youth, such as nurses, because underresourcing could have consequences for the general student population. Deborah McMahan, Health Commissioner of Fort Wayne-Allen County Department of Health, confirmed that almost half of Burmese refugees screened have latent tuberculosis (TB). According to Dr. McMahan, there is a 10- to 15-percent lifetime risk of developing active TB within this group[13], a disease which is contagious, and one's susceptibility to developing active TB is increased by malnutrition and a weak immune system—each being prevalent among refugees. On average, as noted by the World Health Organization, each person with active TB infects 10–15 people before antibiotics, and isolation procedures render them noncontagious.[14] Dr. McMahan contended that if 50 percent of the roughly 800 refugees resettled in 2008 are assumed to have latent

---

[11] The five schools are Southwick Elementary School, Meadow Brooke Elementary School, Village Elementary School, Prince Chapman Middle School, and Paul Harding High School.
[12] The two schools are South Side High School and North Side High School.
[13] The World Health Organization notes that 5–10 percent of people in general who are infected with TB become sick or infectious. Available at http://who.int/mediacentre/factsheets/fs104/en/index.html.
[14] Id.

TB, the city could have as many as 100 to 200 new cases of active TB within the Burmese population alone. In the absence of effective monitoring and treatment, this could present a significant threat to public health.

Nancy Chamberlin, Deputy Chief of police in Fort Wayne, expressed concern for the safety of her officers who face the risk of exposure to TB when responding to situations within the Burmese community. She also referenced alarming incidents regarding elevated rates of violence and exploitation faced by women and children—citing a recent case in which a 50-year-old Burmese man was found offering the sexual services of a 14-year-old female relative. Generally, she noted that many refugees are distrustful of officers due to previous experiences of persecution in their countries of origin and do not understand basic laws or social norms.

Dr. McMahan also noted that prearrival health screenings no longer included HIV/AIDS testing, which she identified as very concerning given the elevated rates of infection sometimes found in refugee camps. Prior knowledge of HIV status, she explained, allows for better planning for the complicated care that refugees with such conditions require. Increasingly, the costs of these tests are being dropped on the laps of local and state governments.

She further noted that PRM provides no prearrival population assessments or indicators to aid her in identifying the needs of the refugee groups the city resettles. The discovery of elevated occurrences of hepatitis B among the Burmese population, for example, was cited as a condition she simply "stumbled" upon. The expensive treatment associated with this life-long condition presents another significant cost the local community will be forced to bear.

Totally neglected, she continued, is funding to combat substance abuse, depression, and post-traumatic stress disorder as well as chronic health conditions like obesity, malnutrition, and hypertension—all of which disproportionately plague this population. The issue of inadequate funding for mental health treatment was underscored in the study by the Georgetown Law Human Rights Institute:

> [I]n many cases, refugees' health needs remain untreated, compromising their ability to lead healthy, functional lives. In San Diego, for example, refugees with lingering mental health problems can wait 2 months before seeing a doctor. Similarly, torture treatment centers in the 8 States with the highest number of Iraqi refugee arrivals are experiencing waitlists for services. Other areas where Iraqi refugees are expected to resettle in greater numbers, such as Idaho, Tennessee, and upstate New York, do not have any dedicated torture treatment centers and will therefore require additional funding for training and capacity-building.[15]

The complex nature of assistance required by some refugees, in States across the country, is seriously overstretched or not in place at all.

---

[15] Adess, S. et al. (2009). "Refugee Crisis in America: Iraqis and Their Resettlement Experience." Washington, DC: Georgetown Law Human Rights Institute. Available at www.law.georgetown.edu/news/.../RefugeeCrisisinAmerica_000.pdf.

Case Study: Clarkston, GA

A page one New York Times article published in January 2007 by Warren St. John, which thrust the challenges confronting Clarkston, GA, into the foreground of national discussion, helped bring attention to the burdens many other cities across the United States are also attempting to address.[16] The article described deeply concerning stories of prejudice, police brutality, and a small community of roughly 7,000 that was shattered under the pressure of a broken refugee resettlement system.

However, the tensions highlighted in the article between the refugee population and most long-time residents, according to the Clarkston's former mayor, were not inflamed by deep-seeded prejudice, but were rooted in the fact that resettlement agencies completely failed to warn the city that refugees would be placed in their community. When asked if city officials were consulted, Mayor Lee Swaney stated, "We were not part of the process of bringing them here. We were told after the fact that they were coming." He argued that settling refugees in Clarkston, without coordinating with the city, left him with the lion's share of responsibility but no voice. In addition, refugees placed excessive burdens on already scarce resources because he claimed the city did not receive extra money to address the special needs of this population.

In April 2003, Georgia Representative Karla Drenner, whose district includes Clarkston, in response to concerns articulated by constituents like Mayor Swaney, introduced legislation that would have compelled voluntary agencies working in the State to report to government authorities whenever 10 or more refugees were resettled in a municipality.[17] This past year, she also convened a townhall meeting where she publicly encouraged the voluntary agencies located within the city to improve communication with elected officials and to provide more warning regarding when refugees were due to arrive. The current mayor of Clarkston, Howard Tygrett, reported that all of the resettlement agencies subsequently relocated outside of the city limits in order to circumvent this appeal and that communication has not improved since he assumed office roughly one year ago.

From the perspective of the resettlement agencies, Clarkston offered refugees the basic services needed to gather their bearings and get on their feet, which was their primary concern. The convenient access to the metro-Atlanta job market, nearby highway system, and affordable housing that made the city ideal for long-time residents were the factors that caused Clarkston to be selected as the primary resettlement city for all of Georgia.

Since the most immediate challenge faced by refugees after arriving was finding employment as a means to reach self-sufficiency, living in Clarkston made sense. Although Clarkston's business sector, comprised largely of small businesses, could not provide enough jobs, refugees had access to the city of Atlanta. Resettle-

---

[16] See appendix V. Warren St. John. "Refugees Find Hostility and Hope on Soccer Field." New York Times 21 Jan. 2007. Available at http://www.nytimes.com/2007/01/21/us/21fugees.html?ex=1327035600&en=a213425fdcd1892f&ei=5088&partner=rssnyt&emc=rss.

[17] 17 See Appendix VI. Legislation introduced in the Georgia General Assembly as House Bill 1002 by Representative Karla Drenner, April 2003. Available at http://www.legis.state.ga.us/legis/2003_04/versions/hb1002_LC_28_1311_a_2.htm.

ment agencies thought that the low-skill jobs most refugee adults qualified for, because of their limited English and educational backgrounds, would be available in Atlanta.

After finding work, however, figuring out how to get there every day became the next problem. As the former mayor noted:

> Transportation was a big issue and I can understand why. If you get a job, but can't get there you are no better off. So transportation was a big issue. Catching MARTA, it played a big role because it was convenient.

MARTA, the public transportation system connecting Clarkston to the larger Atlanta area, made travel to work possible for struggling refugees unable to afford private vehicles.

The abundance of affordable housing in Clarkston was identified by the resettlement agencies as the best option for refugees who needed the jobs available in Atlanta but could not afford its more expensive rent. Overbuilding during the 1980s created a situation in which the housing ratio was 80 percent multidwelling and 20 percent single-dwelling. Thus, Clarkston's apartments became home to refugees who for too long lived in the squalor of refugee camps.

Each of these factors were important for helping refugees get on their feet, but the citizens of Clarkston were often left to deal with the problems that emerged long after the resettlement agencies were gone. To illustrate this point, the former mayor discussed the living conditions of some refugee families he observed who were unaccustomed to living in the apartments they were placed in. Mayor Swaney stated:

> I know that when the health department and I went into some of these apartments you would not believe what we saw. They had no idea how to live in one of these places and I fault the agencies that brought them here. If they come and they know what a toilet is for and they know what a faucet and gas stove is then they fit in to how we live here.

Further, when accidental fires were caused by inappropriate handling of household appliances, the burden fell on Clarkston's police department to deal with the emotional and structural damage. The deaths of four refugee youth, who were killed during a tragic apartment fire in 2008, underscored this point.

The former mayor contended that the collective burden of these issues caused resentment among some long-time residents. He cited many meetings he attended to discuss his grievances and to petition for these problems to be addressed by the resettlement agencies, but no action was taken because the agencies claimed to be financially constrained themselves.

Between 1996 and 2001, nearly 20,000 refugees were sent to Georgia, and with most resettling in Clarkston or the surrounding areas, nearly half of the city's population were foreign-born or refugee at any given time.[18] The current vice mayor, Emanuel Ransom, offered an anecdotal example in stating, "I am there most

---
[18] Id.

days court is held and 90 percent of the local people in the court cannot speak English."

The larger ramifications of the strain associated with the resettlement process are best illustrated by focusing on the public school system in Clarkston. Teachers and administrators are said to be failing to address the special needs of the refugee youth, in addition to the needs of the general student population. Consequently, the deteriorating condition of overall instruction has fuelled significant shifts in the demographics of Clarkston's population.

The reaction of many long-time residents of Clarkston to the increasing pressures placed on the educational system was simply to relocate. Regarding the state of Clarkston's schools, Luma Mufleh, a community advocate on behalf of refugees in Clarkston, remarked:

> I think it's unfair for the government to put a ton of refugees in a city and not equip them with the resources to handle them. The schools are all failing. Every school in Clarkston is failing because schools are not equipped to handle this. A teacher cannot teach 10 kids at 10 different levels. So, I understand their frustration, but they need to come up with solutions. All the white people have left because no one wants their child to receive a bad education. I have lots of friends who would be interested in moving to Clarkston because of the diversity the city offers, but only if they are single. My married friends would not think of moving here because of the schools. They would not want to put their kids in Clarkston's schools. So they have to start with the schools because that is the biggest issue.

The resettlement process was contributing to divisions and resentment between refugee and nonrefugee populations in Clarkston. Further, because refugees lacked the means to move their families to cities with better schools, their children received what she believed to be second-rate educations and limited long-term options.

While a local pastor noted that the flight of some long-time Clarkston residents was driven by a desire to avoid the diverse populations entering the city, he cited firsthand experience of how important a consideration quality schools were for families with children. Pastor Phil Kitchen of Clarkston International Bible Church decided to register his own children in a different school system because of the horror stories he heard about Clarkston upon accepting the pastorate of his church. As his family prepared to relocate, he recalled several of the selectors on the church's search committee strongly advising him against considering Clarkston's schools because of their deplorable condition. The pastor stated:

> I remember talking with them and they recommended that I keep my kids out of Clarkston's schools. So my wife and I decided to live in the city a few miles away for the sake of our family. Every parent wants their child to receive the best education available and the simple fact is that the kids in Clarkston are at a disadvantage.

According to recently released results from Georgia's statewide standardized math exam for the 2009–10 academic year, Clarkston High School has the highest percentage of failing scores of all metro-Atlanta schools—with 47.8 percent of students reported as failing.[19]

Conclusion

The American people have generously welcomed far more refugees than all other countries and we are a richer society for having embraced such diverse cultures. While offering safe haven to persecuted populations throughout the world remains a humanitarian imperative, the administration should avoid biting off more than local communities are capable of chewing. Especially in a difficult economic climate, force-feeding refugees into a broken system is proving to be detrimental to the longer term interests of refugees and to the cities that receive them.

The U.S. resettlement program should be perceived as a benefit to local communities, not a burden. To the extent that the resettlement cities included in this report are building intercultural bridges and making the system work, it often appears to occur in spite of government resources and not because of them. Best articulated by Senator Edward Kennedy in a 1981 report discussing the Refugee Act of 1980—legislation he authored—he argued that the administration and Congress should ensure local communities are not negatively impacted by "programs they did not initiate and for which they were not responsible."[20] Immediate action is required to make this a reality today.

---

[19] D. Aileen Dodd and John Perry. "New Curriculum: Math Anxiety for Students and Teachers." The Atlanta Journal-Constitution, 20 May 2010. Available at http://www.ajc.com/news/new-curriculum-math-anxiety-532073.html.

[20] Kennedy, E. M. (1981). "Refugee Act of 1980." International Migration Review, Vol. 15, No. ½ Refugees Today (Spring-Summer, 1981).

ACKNOWLEDGEMENTS

The following contributed in some way to the preparation of this report, or continue to assist the committee with this ongoing project.

U.S. Government:
- National Security Council
- Department of Health and Human Services
- Department of State

Individuals:
- Susan Boyle, Former State Refugee Coordinator, State of Indiana
- Jay Branegan, Senate Foreign Relations Committee
- Susan Brouillette, Senator Lugar's Office, Indianapolis, Indiana
- Nancy Chamberlin, Deputy Chief, Southeast Division, Fort Wayne Police Department
- Meg Distler, St. Joseph Community Health Foundation, Fort Wayne, Indiana
- Karla Drenner, Georgia House of Representatives, State of Georgia
- Cathy Gallmeyer, Senator Lugar's Office, Fort Wayne, Indiana
- Palermo Galindo, Hispanic and Immigrant Liaison, Fort Wayne, Indiana
- Mark GiaQuinta, President, Fort Wayne Community Schools
- Fred Gilbert, Social Worker, Fort Wayne Indiana
- David Gogol, Vice-Chair, B&D Consulting
- Joe Johns, Director of Missional Living, Fellowship Missionary Church, Fort Wayne, Indiana
- Emily Keirns Schwartz, Coordinator, English language Learners (ELL), Fort Wayne Community Schools
- Phil Kitchin, Pastor, Clarkston International Bible Church
- Desiree Koger-Gustafson, Staff Attorney, Neighborhood Christian Legal Clinic
- Keith Luse, Senate Foreign Relations Committee
- Dr. Deborah McMahan, Commissioner, Fort Wayne-Allen County Department of Health
- Luma Mufleh, CEO and Coach, Fugees Family
- Jim Murua, Assistant Chief Fire Marshal, City of Fort Wayne
- Emanuel Ransom, Vice-Mayor, City of Clarkston
- Wendy Robinson, Superintendent, Fort Wayne Community Schools
- Debbie Schmidt, Executive Director, Catholic Charities
- Tony Scipio, Chief of Police, City of Clarkston
- Lee Swaney, Former Mayor, City of Clarkston
- Minn Myint Nan Tin, Burmese Advocacy Center, Fort Wayne, Indiana
- Helen Townsend, Refugee Health Coordinator, State of Indiana
- Howard Tygrett, Mayor, City of Clarkston
- Monica Vela, Refuge Support/ELL Liaison, Fort Wayne Community Schools

- Becky Weimerskirch, Executive Director, Community Transportation Network, Inc.
- Bernard White L. III, Licensed Special Education Teacher, Paul Harding High School
- Ocleva Williams, Neighborhood Action Center, Autumn Woods
- Dr. Julie Zehr, Assistant Superintendent, East Allen County Schools

APPENDIX I

SUMMARY OF REFUGEE ADMISSIONS AS OF 30 APRIL 2010

Department of State
Bureau of Population, Refugees, and Migration
Office of Admissions – Refugee Processing Center
Summary of Refugee Admissions
as of 30-April-2010

Cumulative Summary of Refugee Admissions

Fiscal Year	Africa	Asia	Europe	Former Soviet Union	Kosovo	Latin America Caribbean	Near East South Asia	PSI	Total
1975	0	135,000	1,947	6,211	0	3,000	0	0	146,158
1976	0	15,000	1,756	7,450	0	3,000	0	0	27,206
1977	0	7,000	1,755	8,191	0	3,000	0	0	19,946
1978	0	20,574	2,245	10,688	0	3,050	0	0	36,567
1979	0	76,521	3,393	24,449	0	7,000	0	0	111,363
1980	955	163,799	5,025	28,444	0	6,662	2,231	0	207,116
1981	2,119	131,139	6,704	13,444	0	2,017	3,829	0	159,252
1982	3,412	73,795	11,108	2,780	0	580	6,485	0	98,096
1983	2,648	39,245	11,867	1,342	0	671	1,429	0	61,218
1984	2,747	51,678	10,096	721	0	160	4,659	0	70,393
1985	1,951	49,962	9,233	625	0	161	5,764	0	67,704
1986	1,322	48,482	8,503	798	0	131	3,609	0	62,146
1987	1,980	40,089	8,386	3,699	0	328	10,031	0	64,528
1988	1,693	35,371	7,310	20,411	0	2,497	8,366	733	76,460
1989	1,952	46,722	8,763	39,602	0	2,604	6,639	1,550	107,070
1990	3,453	51,598	6,994	50,526	0	2,326	4,979	3,004	122,066
1991	4,420	53,522	6,833	38,226	0	2,263	5,343	1,768	113,389
1992	5,479	51,869	2,913	61,397	0	3,063	8,000	60	132,531
1993	6,967	49,817	2,582	48,773	0	4,071	6,037	281	118,448
1994	5,860	43,564	7,709	43,864	0	6,156	3,940	0	112,981
1995	4,827	36,987	10,070	35,951	0	7,026	4,118	0	98,974
1996	7,604	19,321	12,145	29,816	0	3,560	1,867	0	74,293
1997	6,028	8,694	21,405	27,331	0	2,968	4,101	0	70,488
1998	6,887	10,654	30,842	23,587	0	1,627	3,318	0	77,095
1999	13,043	10,206	24,499	17,410	14,161	2,118	4,086	0	85,523
2000	17,561	4,561	22,561	15,103	0	3,332	10,128	0	73,147
2001	10,021	3,725	15,777	15,748	0	2,973	12,000	0	69,304
2002	2,551	3,512	5,468	9,985	0	1,832	3,750	0	27,119
2003	10,719	1,724	2,399	8,744	0	455	4,260	0	28,404

Data extracted from the Worldwide Refugee Admissions Processing System (WRAPS).

RPCREPORT.STATISTICIAN\REFUGEE ADMISSIONS REPORT
Report Run Date: 5/5/2010 9:30:40 AM

Page 1 of 2

Department of State
Bureau of Population, Refugees, and Migration
Office of Admissions - Refugee Processing Center
Summary of Refugee Admissions
as of 30-April-2010

Year									
2004	29,104	8,084 *	489	8,765	0	3,577	2,854	0	52,977
2005	20,745	12,076 *	11,316	0	0	6,698	2,072	0	53,818
2006	18,126	5,659 *	10,468	0	0	3,264	3,716	0	41,223
2007	17,465	15,643 *	4,891	0	0	2,970	7,619	0	48,281
2008	8,935	19,409 *	2,344	0	0	4,777	25,147	0	60,191
2009	9,670	18,850 *	1,997	0	0	4,851	38,375	0	74,654
2010	6,038	9,926	977	0	0	2,945	21,775	0	41,596
Total	245,183	1,371,358	301,623	695,166	14,161	167,753	242,192	8,274	2,895,711

* Includes Amerasian Immigrants

Data extracted from the Worldwide Refugee Admissions Processing System (WRAPS).

RPGREPORT STATISTICIAN/REFUGEE ADMISSIONS REPORT
Report Run Date: 5/5/2010 9:30:40 AM

APPENDIX II

Official Letter From City of Fort Wayne, IN

City of Fort Wayne
THOMAS C. HENRY, MAYOR

November 7, 2008

Mr. Mitch Roob
Secretary
Family Social Services Administration
State of Indiana
402 W Washington St, Room W461
Indianapolis, IN 46204

Dear Mitch:

On behalf of the Fort Wayne community, thank you again for your leadership and assistance with regards to our Burmese refugee situation. The solutions you proposed have gotten off to a great start, and we are grateful for your help.

Unfortunately, our fundamental challenge remains. How will this community cope with the costs and challenges of continued high levels of Burmese refugee relocation? Fort Wayne has opened its arms to refugees for the past 20 years and will continue accepting them if the community as a whole is able to serve them. But since September 2007, Fort Wayne has been the recipient of nearly 1,400 Burmese primary refugees and a significant number of secondary migrants. The dramatic increase in the pace of resettlement has placed a significant burden on our community.

Our local resettlement agency, Catholic Charities, works hard to provide for the refugees during their first few months in the US, and even after their contractual obligations end, assists the Burmese with housing and access to services. But following the first six months, the burden of assimilation, care, and absorption falls on the community—schools, hospitals, numerous nonprofits, and the City must step up and assume the costs to assure that this vulnerable population succeed in their new city. We have evaluated our capacity and have realized that the community will not be able to provide services if the current pace of resettlement continues. For example, the local medical community has established that their capacity to provide the necessary health screenings and care to the refugees is limited to 700 individuals per year—which leaves refugees vulnerable to disease and the community vulnerable to public health risks.

The recent numbers of incoming refugees has significantly strained our resources, and as such, I request that you help us work to slow the pace of resettlement to Fort Wayne. We have been informed by Catholic Charities and World Relief that they anticipate 750-900 new refugees this year and more into the future. The community cannot accommodate that level of resettlement, nor can it absorb 75 refugees per week, which has been a common occurrence. It is my understanding that the State Refugee Coordinator plays a key role for the United States Department of State in assessing a community's capacity to resettle refugees. It is my hope that

SAFE CITY · QUALITY JOBS · B.E.S.T.
One Main St. · Fort Wayne, Indiana · 46802-1804 · www.cityoffortwayne.org
An Equal Opportunity Employer

the Indiana State Coordinator will inform the State Department that the Fort Wayne community is overburdened and overwhelmed. Enclosed you will find a copy of the minutes from the Immigrant Refugee Area Executives Meeting held on Thursday, October 30, 2008 which identifies the challenges that our community is facing.

I hope that with your guidance and assistance of your staff, we can work to convince the State Department to reduce the flow of refugees to northeastern Indiana. On behalf of the Fort Wayne community, I appreciate your attention to our challenges and look forward to working with you to improve the resettlement process for this vulnerable population.

Sincerely,

Thomas C. Henry
City of Fort Wayne
Mayor

Sincerely yours in our Lord,

Most Reverend John M. D'Arcy
Diocese of Fort Wayne-South Bend

encl.

cc: Senator Evan Bayh
Senator Richard Lugar
Congressman Mark Souder

APPENDIX III

Refugee Article in The News-Sentinel

"No Burmese" Sign Draws Ire Despite Business Owner's Apology, City's Civil-Rights Watchdog Is Investigating

(By Kevin Leininger)

Some of their customers' actions, management says, were "alarming."

But by targeting an entire ethnic group instead of the unacceptable behavior, an employee's sign has forced the Anderson-based owner of a local business to apologize and drawn the attention of the city's civil-rights watchdog.

"For sanitary reasons, there are no Burmese people allowed," read the sign that was posted on the door of Ricker Oil Co.'s coin-operated laundry on South Calhoun Street near Rudisill Boulevard—until an irate passerby alerted the offices of the Burmese Advocacy Center, 2826 S. Calhoun St., and the Neighborhood Christian Legal Clinic, igniting a firestorm of protest in the media and on the Internet culminating in Tuesday's apology from President Jay Ricker.

"Unfortunately, an employee responded to an alarming situation in an appropriate manner . . . the sign in question was removed, and we are exploring appropriate disciplinary action," Ricker said in a statement. "It is the policy of Ricker's to welcome all patrons to its facilities. We are committed to maintaining a positive relationship with all members of the communities we serve." Ricker's, founded in 1979, has more than 700 employees and operates 49 convenience stores and two laundries.

Desiree Koger-Gustafson, attorney for the legal clinic that serves mostly low-income and immigrant clients, said she was going to protest the sign, but its removal and the apology were sufficient for her to drop the matter.

"Someone should inform (whoever wrote the sign) of the last few decades of civil-rights laws. Some people still think you can do this kind of thing," she said.

Gerald Foday isn't one of those people, however. The director of Fort Wayne's Metropolitan Human Relations Commission said his agency may file a complaint, and could pursue civil-rights charges against Ricker's if an investigation warrants it. Sanctions could include fines, mandatory employee training and other remedies, he said.

"You can sanction behavior based on health," he said—but you can't banish an entire group based on the actions of certain individuals.

Ricker's spokesman Jonathan Bausman did not want to elaborate on the behaviors resulting in the sign. "We don't want it to seem like we're trying to justify it," he said.

But signs still posted at the laundry in English and Burmese offer a clue: "No spitting! No betel nut!" they read.

According to Koger-Gustafson, many Burmese chew betel nut, which is common in their country of Burma, or Myanmar as it's called by the ruling junta, and spit the residue, which can result in red stains. Bausman said Ricker's has discussed its concerns about certain behaviors with Burmese advocates and the Fort Wayne-Allen County Department of Health, and said other companies have expressed similar concerns.

Health department spokesman John Silcox said there are "ongoing issues about what can and can't be tolerated" with newly arriving immigrant and refugee groups, especially in the area of hygiene. Fort Wayne is home to about 5,000 Burmese—the largest concentration in the United States.

The sign's removal and Ricker's apology don't satisfy all Burmese.

Kyaw Soe, who came to Fort Wayne from Burma in 1993 and is director of IPFW's New Immigrant Literacy Program, visited the laundry Tuesday and said he still considers it an unfriendly place for Burmese.

"Therre were signs (in Burmese prohibiting certain actions) in every room. There were 22 in Burmese to only one in Spanish. It's nonverbal behavior that is non-welcoming. We need more education, more cultural sensitivity."

Those signs about not using betel nut apparently didn't originate with Ricker's, however. Koger-Gustafson said they were provided by the Burmese Advocacy Center.

In fact, one was posted Tuesday atop the counter at the group's office.

APPENDIX IV

Refugee Article in The Journal Gazette

Burmese Demand Action on Prejudice See Official Indifference To Sign at Laundry

(By Devon Haynie)

Dozens of shivering Burmese gathered in front of the Courthouse on Sunday to urge government officials to publicly denounce discrimination against their community.

Organizers said the rally was a response to the government's lack of reaction to a controversial sign posted at Ricker's City Laundry on South Calhoun Street several weeks ago. The sign, which has since been removed, read, "For Sanitary Purposes, There Are No Burmese People Allowed." Jay Ricker, head of the company, has since apologized for the sign, but Burmese at the rally said it was not enough to ease their fears of continued discrimination.

"The government has been silent," said Maung Maung Soe, one of the event's organizers. "If the government does not take action, we will take legal action."

Details surrounding the sign remain unclear. But by all accounts, it seems that a lone employee posted it, perhaps in response to the Burmese tradition of chewing betel nuts and spitting out the juice. Ricker posted an apology on Facebook and read an apology in a video posted on YouTube.

At the rally, members of the Burmese community held signs reading "We Want Equal Rights" and "We Are Burmese Americans." Organizers said they planned to stage a larger rally in a few days, but had to keep the gathering small because they hadn't received a permit.

Fort Wayne is home to about 5,500 people from Myanmar, formerly known as Burma. Many are legal refugees who fled the country to escape the country's 60-year civil war.

"We aren't foreigners coming to visit; we are citizens," said Nyan Aung, an event organizer who has lived in the United States since 1993. "We need to be treated more like other people. (People) need to respect our human rights."

Thandar Thet, a 15-year-old sophomore at North Side High School, came to the rally with her father and 5-year-old brother. She said the sign posting made her feel uneasy about her future in Fort Wayne.

"I've never been discriminated against, but I don't believe this is right," Thet said. "My parents came to America for freedom. They talked about discrimination in Burma, but that is what we came here to escape."

APPENDIX V

Refugee Article in The New York Times

[From the New York Times, Jan. 21, 2007]

Refugees Find Hostility and Hope on Soccer Field

(By Warren St. John)

Editors' Note Appended
Correction Appended

CLARKSTON, GA., Jan. 20.—Early last summer the mayor of this small town east of Atlanta issued a decree: no more soccer in the town park.

"There will be nothing but baseball down there as long as I am mayor," Lee Swaney, a retired owner of a heating and air-conditioning business, told the local paper. "Those fields weren't made for soccer."

In Clarkston, soccer means something different than in most places. As many as half the residents are refugees from war-torn countries around the world. Placed by resettlement agencies in a once mostly white town, they receive 90 days of assistance from the government and then are left to fend for themselves. Soccer is their game.

But to many longtime residents, soccer is a sign of unwanted change, as unfamiliar and threatening as the hijabs worn by the Muslim women in town. It's not football. It's not baseball. The fields weren't made for it. Mayor Swaney even has a name for the sort of folks who play the game: the soccer people.

Caught in the middle is a boys soccer program called the Fugees—short for refugees, though most opponents guess the name refers to the hip-hop band.

The Fugees are indeed all refugees, from the most troubled corners—Afghanistan, Bosnia, Burundi, Congo, Gambia, Iraq, Kosovo, Liberia, Somalia and Sudan. Some have endured unimaginable hardship to get here: squalor in refugee camps, separation from siblings and parents. One saw his father killed in their home.

The Fugees, 9 to 17 years old, play on three teams divided by age. Their story is about children with miserable pasts trying to make good with strangers in a very different and sometimes hostile place. But as a season with the youngest of the three teams revealed, it is also a story about the challenges facing resettled refugees in this country. More than 900,000 have been admitted to the United States since 1993, and their presence seems to bring out the best in some people and the worst in others.

The Fugees' coach exemplifies the best. A woman volunteering in a league where all the other coaches are men, some of them paid former professionals from Europe, she spends as much time helping her players' families make new lives here as coaching soccer.

At the other extreme are some town residents, opposing players and even the parents of those players, at their worst hurling racial epithets and making it clear they resent the mostly African team. In a region where passions run high on the subject of illegal immigration, many are unaware or unconcerned that, as refugees, the Fugees are here legally.

"There are no gray areas with the Fugees," said the coach, Luma Mufleh. "They trigger people's reactions on class, on race. They speak with accents and don't seem American. A lot of people get shaken up by that."

LOTS OF RUNNING, MANY RULES

The mayor's soccer ban has everything to do with why, on a scorching August afternoon, Ms. Mufleh—or Coach Luma, as she is known in the refugee community—is holding tryouts for her under-13 team on a rutted, sand-scarred field behind an elementary school.

The boys at the tryouts wear none of the shiny apparel or expensive cleats common in American youth soccer. One plays in ankle-high hiking boots, some in baggy jeans, another in his socks. On the barren lot, every footfall and pivot produces a puff of chalky dust that hangs in the air like fog.

Across town, the lush field in Milam Park sits empty.

Ms. Mufleh blows her whistle.

"Listen up," she tells the panting and dusty boys. "I don't care how well you play. I care how hard you work. Every Monday and Wednesday, I'm going to have you from 5 to 8." The first half will be for homework and tutoring. Ms. Mufleh has arranged volunteers for that. The second half will be for soccer, and for running. Lots of running.

"If you miss a practice, you miss the next game," she tells the boys. "If you miss two games, you're off the team."

The final roster will be posted on the bulletin board at the public library by 10 Friday morning, she says. Don't bother to call.

And one more thing. She holds up a stack of paper, contracts she expects her players to sign. "If you can't live with this," she says, "I don't want you on this team."

Hands—black, brown, white—reach for the paper. As the boys read, eyes widen:

I will have good behavior on and off the field.
I will not smoke.
I will not do drugs.
I will not drink alcohol.
I will not get anyone pregnant.
I will not use bad language.
My hair will be shorter than Coach's.
I will be on time.
I will listen to Coach.
I will try hard.
I will ask for help.
I want to be part of the Fugees!

A TOWN TRANSFORMED

Until the refugees began arriving, the mayor likes to say, Clarkston "was just a sleepy little town by the railroad tracks."

Since then, this town of 7,100 has become one of the most diverse communities in America.

Clarkston High School now has students from more than 50 countries. The local mosque draws more than 800 to Friday prayers. There is a Hindu temple, and there are congregations of Vietnamese, Sudanese and Liberian Christians.

At the shopping center, American stores have been displaced by Vietnamese, Ethiopian and Eritrean restaurants and a halal butcher. The only hamburger joint in town, City Burger, is run by an Iraqi.

The transformation began in the late 1980s, when resettlement agencies, private groups that contract with the federal government, decided Clarkston was perfect for refugees to begin new lives. The town had an abundance of inexpensive apartments, vacated by middle-class whites who left for more affluent suburbs. It had public transportation; the town was the easternmost stop on the Atlanta rail system. And it was within commuting distance of downtown Atlanta's booming economy, offering new arrivals at least the prospect of employment.

At first the refugees—most from Southeast Asia—arrived so slowly that residents barely noticed. But as word got out about Clarkston's suitability, more agencies began placing refugees here. From 1996 to 2001, more than 19,000 refugees from around the world resettled in Georgia, many in Clarkston and surrounding DeKalb County, to the dismay of many longtime residents.

Many of those residents simply left. Others stayed but remained resentful, keeping score of the ways they thought the refugees were altering their lives. There were events that reinforced fears that Clarkston was becoming unsafe: a mentally ill Sudanese boy beheaded his 5-year-old cousin in their Clarkston apartment; a fire in a crowded apartment in town claimed the lives of four Liberian refugee children.

At a town meeting in 2003 meant to foster understanding between the refugees and residents, the first question, submitted on an index card, was, "What can we do to keep the refugees from coming to Clarkston?"

A COACH WITH A PASSION

Luma Mufleh, 31, says she was born to coach. She grew up in Amman, Jordan, in a Westernized family, and attended the American Community School, for American and European expatriates and a few well-to-do Jordanians. There, Muslim girls were free to play sports as boys did, and women were permitted to coach.

Her mentor was an American volleyball coach who demanded extreme loyalty and commitment. Ms. Mufleh picked up on a paradox. Though she claimed to dislike her coach, she wanted to play well for her.

"For the majority of the time she coached me, I hated her," Ms. Mufleh said. "But she had our respect. Until then, I'd always played for me. I'd never played for a coach."

Ms. Mufleh attended college in the United States, in part because she felt women here had more opportunities. She went to Smith College, and after graduation moved to Atlanta. She soon found her first coaching job, as head of a 12-and-under girls soccer team through the local Y.M.C.A.

On the field, Ms. Mufleh emulated her volleyball coach, an approach that did not always sit well with American parents. When she ordered her players to practice barefoot, to get a better feel for the soccer ball, a player's mother objected on the grounds that her daughter could injure her toes.

"This is how I run my practice," Ms. Mufleh told her. "If she's not going to do it, she's not going to play."

Ms. Mufleh's first team lost every game. But over time her methods paid off. Her players returned. They got better. In her third season, her team was undefeated.

When Ms. Mufleh learned about the growing refugee community in Clarkston, she floated the idea of starting a soccer program. The Y.M.C.A. offered to back her with uniforms and equipment. So in the summer of 2004, Ms. Mufleh made fliers announcing tryouts in Arabic, English, French and Vietnamese and distributed them around apartment complexes where the refugees lived.

For a coach hoping to build a soccer program in Clarkston, the biggest challenge was not finding talented players. There were plenty of those, boys who had learned the game in refugee camps in Africa and in parking lots around town. The difficulty was finding players who would show up.

Many of the players come from single-parent families, with mothers or fathers who work hours that do not sync with sports schedules. Few refugee families own cars. Players would have to be self-sufficient.

On a June afternoon, 23 boys showed up for the tryouts.

From the beginning, the players were wary. A local church offered a free basketball program for refugee children largely as a cover for missionary work.

Others simply doubted that a woman could coach soccer.

"She's a girl—she doesn't know what she's talking about," Ms. Mufleh overheard a Sudanese boy say at an early practice.

She ordered him to stand in the goal. As the team watched, she blasted a shot directly at the boy, who dove out of the way.

"Anybody else?" she asked.

IN BRUTAL PASTS, A BOND

Jeremiah Ziaty, one of those early players, is a typical member of the Fugees.

In 1997, in the midst of Liberia's 14 years of civil war, rebels led by Charles Taylor showed up one night at the Ziatys' house in Monrovia. Jeremiah's father was a low-level worker in a government payroll office. The rebels thought he had money. When they learned he did not, they killed him in the family's living room.

Beatrice Ziaty, Jeremiah's mother, grabbed her sons and fled out the back door. The Ziatys trekked through the bush for a week until they reached a refugee camp in the Ivory Coast. There, they lived in a mud hut and scavenged for food. After five years in the camp, Ms. Ziaty learned her family had been accepted for resettlement in Clarkston, a town she had never heard of.

The United States Committee for Refugees and Immigrants in Washington estimates that there are now more than 12 million refugees worldwide and more than 20 million people displaced within their own nations' borders. In 2005, only 80,800 were accepted by other nations for resettlement, according to the United Nations.

The Ziatys' resettlement followed a familiar script. The family was lent $3,016 for one-way airline tickets to the United States, which they repaid in three years. After a two-day journey from Abidjan, they were greeted in Atlanta by a case worker from the International Rescue Committee, a resettlement organization. She took them to an apartment in Clarkston where the cupboard had been stocked with canned goods.

The case worker helped Ms. Ziaty find a job, as a maid at the Ritz-Carlton Hotel in the affluent Buckhead section of Atlanta, one that required an hour commute by bus. While walking home from the bus stop after her first day, Ms. Ziaty was mugged and her purse stolen.

Terrified of her new surroundings, Ms. Ziaty told her son Jeremiah never to leave the house. Like any 8-year-old, Jeremiah bristled. He especially wanted to play soccer. Through friends in the neighborhood, he heard about tryouts for the Fugees.

"When he tell me, 'Mom, I go play soccer,' I tell him he's too small, don't go out of the house," Ms. Ziaty recalled. "Then he would start crying."

Ms. Ziaty relaxed her rule when she met Ms. Mufleh, who promised to take care of her son.

That was three years ago. At age 11, Jeremiah is a leader of the 13-and-under Fugees, shifting among sweeper, center midfielder and center forward.

Other members of the Fugees also have harrowing stories. Qendrim Bushi's Muslim family fled Kosovo when Serbian soldiers torched his father's grocery store and threatened to kill them. Eldin Subasic's uncle was shot in Bosnia. And so on.

The Fugees, Ms. Mufleh believed, shared something intense. They knew trauma. They knew the fear and loneliness of the newcomer. This was their bond.

"In order to get a group to work together, to be effective together, you have to find what is common," she said. "The refugee experience is pretty powerful."

* * * * * * *

Ms. Mufleh made a point never to ask her players about their pasts. On the soccer field, she felt, refugees should leave that behind.

Occasionally, though, a boy would reveal a horrific memory. One reported that he had been a child soldier. When she expressed frustration that a Liberian player tuned out during practice, another Liberian told her she didn't understand: the boy had been forced by soldiers to shoot his best friend.

"It was learning to not react," Ms. Mufleh said. "I just wanted to listen. How do you respond when a kid says, 'I saw my dad shot in front of me'? I didn't know."

As a Jordanian in the Deep South, Ms. Mufleh identified in some ways with the refugees. A legal resident awaiting a green card, she often felt an outsider herself, and knew what it was like to be far from home.

She also found she was needed. Her fluent Arabic and conversational French came in handy for players' mothers who needed to translate a never-ending flow of government paperwork. Teachers learned to call her when her players' parents could not be located. Families began to invite her to dinner, platters of rice and bowls of leafy African stews. The Ziatys cut back on the peppers when Coach Luma came over; they learned she couldn't handle them.

Upon hearing of the low wages the refugee women were earning, Ms. Mufleh thought she could do better. She started a house and office cleaning company called Fresh Start, to employ refugee women. The starting salary is $10 an hour, nearly double the minimum wage and more than the women were earning as maids in downtown hotels. She guarantees a 50-cent raise every year, and now employs six refugee women.

Ms. Mufleh said that when she started the soccer program, she was hopelessly naive about how it would change her life.

"I thought I would coach twice a week and on weekends—like coaching other kids," she said. "It's 40 or 60 hours a week—coaching, finding jobs, taking people to the hospital. You start off on your own, and you suddenly have a family of 120."

OFF TO A ROUGH START

On a Friday morning in August, the boys come one by one to look for their names on the roster at the public library. Many go away disappointed, but six do not.

The new players are:

Mohammed Mohammed, 12, a bright-eyed Iraqi Kurd whose family fled Saddam Hussein for Turkey five years ago and who speaks only a few words of English.

Idwar and Robin Dikori, two rocket-fast Sudanese brothers, 12 and 10, who lost their mother, sister and two younger brothers in a car crash after arriving in Clarkston.

Shahir Anwar, 13, an Afghan whose parents fled the Taliban and whose father suffered a debilitating stroke soon after arriving in this country.

Santino Jerke, a shy 11-year-old Sudanese who has just arrived after three years as a refugee in Cairo.

Mafoday Jawneh, a heavyset boy of 12 whose family fell out of favor after a coup in Gambia, and who has a sensitive side; his older brother ribs him for tearing up during "The Oprah Winfrey Show."

Ms. Mufleh is uncertain of her team's prospects. She will have to teach the new players the basics of organized soccer. There are no throw-ins or corner kicks in the street game they have been playing.

In her occasional moments of self-doubt, Ms. Mufleh asks herself: Can I really get these boys to play together? Can I really get them to win?

* * * * * * *

The Fugees' first practice this season is on a sultry August afternoon, with thunderclouds looming in the distance. After 90 minutes of studying, the team runs for half an hour and groans through situps, push-ups and leg lifts.

But the Fugees have no soccer goals. The Y.M.C.A., which sponsors the team, did not place the order, despite a $2,000 grant for the purpose. Ms. Mufleh quietly seethes that a team of wealthy children would probably not have to wait for soccer goals. She likens practice to "playing basketball without a hoop."

The team's first games portend a long season. The Fugees tie their first game, 4–4. In their next game, they surrender a lead and lose, 3–1. The team isn't passing well. Players aren't holding their positions.

On a sweltering afternoon in early September, the Fugees prepare to take the field against the Triumph, a team from nearby Tucker. Even before the game, there is a glaring difference between the Fugees and their competition. The Triumph have brought perhaps 40 parents, siblings and friends, who spread out with folding chairs and picnic blankets and are loaded down with enough energy bars and brightly colored sports drinks for an N.B.A. team.

Though this is technically a home game, no one is on the Fugees' side. During the course of the season, only one Fugees parent will make a game.

The Fugees lead, 2–0, at halftime. In the second half, they put on a show: firing headers, bicycle kicks and a gorgeous arcing shot from 30 yards out. Even the parents of the Triumph gasp and clap in appreciation. At the final whistle, the Fugees have won, 5–1.

"Not bad," Ms. Mufleh tells her team. "But next week will be a much better game, O.K.?"

A CALL FOR CHANGE

Ms. Mufleh has a list of complaints about the Fugees' practice field: little grass, no goals. Neighborhood children regularly wander through the scrimmages, disrupting play.

But after a gang shooting in an apartment complex behind the field in late September, she concludes that the field is not safe. She cancels practice for two days. Fed up, she storms into Mayor Swaney's office, demanding use of the empty field in Milam Park.

When Lee Swaney first ran for City Council in Clarkston more than 15 years ago, he did so as an unabashed representative of "Old Clarkston"—Clarkston before the refugees. It was certainly the more politically viable stance. Because few of the refugees have been in the country long enough to become citizens and vote, political power resides with longtime residents. The 2005 election that gave Mr. Swaney a second four-year term as mayor of this town of 7,100 was determined by just 390 voters.

As mayor, Mr. Swaney has frequently found himself caught between these voters and the thousands of newcomers. But he has also taken potentially unpopular steps on behalf of the refugees. In 2006 he forced the resignation of the town's longtime police chief, in part because of complaints from refugees that Clarkston police officers were harassing them. Mr. Swaney gave the new chief a mandate to purge the Police Department of rogue officers.

Within three months, the chief, a black man of Trinidadian descent named Tony J. Scipio, fired or accepted the resignations of one-third of the force.

Soccer is another matter. Mr. Swaney does not relish his reputation as the mayor who banned soccer. But he must please constituents who complain that refugees are overrunning the town's parks and community center—people like Emanuel Ransom, a black man who moved to Clarkston in the late 1960s.

"A lot of our Clarkston residents are being left out totally," Mr. Ransom says. "Nobody wants to help," he says of the refugees. "It's just, 'Give me, give me, give me.'"

Mr. Swaney encourages Ms. Mufleh to make her case at the next City Council meeting. So in early October she addresses a packed room at City Hall, explaining the team's origins and purpose and promising to pick up trash in the park after practice.

Mr. Swaney takes the floor. He admits concerns about "grown soccer people" who might tear up the field. But these are kids, he says, and "kids are our future."

He announces his support of a six-month trial for the Fugees' use of the field in Milam Park.

The proposal passes unanimously. At least for six months, the Fugees can play on grass.

GETTING BACK IN THE GAME

Early on the morning of Oct. 14, Jeremiah Ziaty is nowhere to be seen. The Fugees have a 9 a.m. game an hour from Clarkston, against the Bluesprings Liberty Fire, one of the top teams. Ms. Mufleh had told her players to meet at the library by 7.

Ms. Mufleh usually leaves players behind if they aren't on time. But she knows Jeremiah's mother is now working nights at a packaging factory; she gets home at 3 a.m. and won't be up to wake Jeremiah. So the coach orders the bus driver to the Ziatys' apartment. Jeremiah is sound asleep. Awakened, he grabs his uniform and fumbles toward the bus.

From the outset of the game, the Fugees, and especially Jeremiah, seem groggy. They fall behind, 1-0. But in the second half, they tie the score, fall behind, and tie it again, 2-2. Jeremiah is now playing fearsome defense. With minutes to go, the Fugees score. They win, 3-2.

"We played as a team," says Qendrim Bushi, the boy from Kosovo. "We didn't yell at each other. Last game, when they scored, all of us were yelling at each other. And Coach made us do a lot of stuff at practice. That's why we win. Only because of Coach."

As the Fugees leave the field, a man on the Bluesprings sideline yells to them, "I'd have paid money to watch that game!"

* * * * * * *

The Fugees have a knack for inspiring such strong reactions, both positive and negative. After one game Ms. Mufleh thought for a moment she was being chased by a rival parent.

"We've heard about your team," the man said when he caught up with her. "We want to know what we can do to help."

The rival team donated cleats, balls and jerseys.

Then there was the game in rural Clarkesville last season at which rival players and even some parents shouted a racial epithet at some of the African players on the Fugees.

After being ejected from a game against the Fugees in November, a rival player made an obscene gesture to nearly every player on the Fugees before heading to his bench. And opponents sometimes mocked the Fugees when they spoke to each other in Swahili, or when Ms. Mufleh shouted instructions in Arabic.

There were even incidents involving referees. Two linesmen were reprimanded by a head referee during a pregame lineup in October for snickering when the name Mohammed Mohammed was called.

Ms. Mufleh tells her players to try their best to ignore these slights. When the other side loses its cool, she tells them, it is a sign of weakness.

Ms. Mufleh is just as fatalistic about bad calls. In her entire coaching career, she tells her players, she has never seen a call reversed because of arguing.

The Fugees are perhaps better equipped to accept this advice than most. Their lives, after all, have been defined by bad calls. On the field, they seem to have a higher threshold for anger than the American players, who often respond to borderline calls as if they are catastrophic injustices. Bad calls, Ms. Mufleh teaches her players, are part of the game. You have to accept them, and move on.

On Oct. 21, Ms. Mufleh is forced to put this theory to the test. The Fugees are on their way to Athens, an hour's drive, for their biggest game, against the undefeated United Gold Valiants. A win will put them in contention for the top spot in their division. Ms. Mufleh sets out in her yellow Volkswagen Beetle, the back seat crammed with balls and cleats. Her team follows in a white Y.M.C.A. bus.

Just outside Monroe, Ms. Mufleh looks to her left and sees a Georgia State Patrol car parallel to her. She looks at her speedometer. She isn't speeding.

The brake light, she thinks.

Ms. Mufleh noticed it early in the week, but between practices, work and evenings shuttling among her players' apartments, she neglected to get it fixed. The trooper turns on his flashing lights. Ms. Mufleh eases to the side and looks at her watch. If this doesn't take too long, the team will make the field in time to warm up.

It isn't so simple. Because of a clerical error, a ticket Ms. Mufleh paid a year before appears unpaid. Her license is suspended. The trooper orders her from her car. In full view of her team, he arrests her.

In the bus, the Fugees become unglued. Santino Jerke, in the country only a few months, begins to weep, violating the unwritten team rule that Fugees don't cry. Several of the Fugees have had family members snatched by uniformed men, just like this. They have been in the United States too little time to understand court dates or bail.

Ms. Mufleh tells the team's manager and bus driver, Tracy Ediger, to take the team to Athens. They know what to do. They can play without her.

Coachless, though, the Fugees are lost. Athens scores within minutes. And scores again. And again. The final score is 5–0.

After the game, Ms. Ediger drives the team back to Monroe. She puts together the $800 bail for Ms. Mufleh and signs some papers. In a few moments, the coach appears. Later, Ms. Mufleh says she thought at that moment about all the times she had told the Fugees to shake off bad calls, to get back in the game, to take responsibility. She walks straight to the bus and her players.

"This was my fault, and I had no excuse for not being there," she tells them. "I should have been there and I wasn't, and the way it happened probably messed you guys up."

Ms. Mufleh asks about the score.

"It was a really hard team, Coach," says Idwar Dikori, the Sudanese speedster.

"Were they better than you?"

"No!" the Fugees shout in unison.

"Come on, guys—were they?"

"No, Coach," Robin Dikori says. "If you were there, we were going to beat them."

Back in Clarkston that night, Ms. Mufleh takes some sweet rolls to the family of Grace Balegamire, a Congolese player. Grace's 9-year-old brother has heard about the arrest, but doesn't believe it.

"If you were in jail," the boy says, "you wouldn't be here."

Ms. Mufleh explains that she gave the people at the jail some money and promised to come back later, so they let her out.

"How much money?" he asks.

"Enough for 500 ice creams."

"If you pay 500 ice creams you can come out of jail?" he asks.

Ms. Mufleh grasps the boy's confusion. The boys' father is a political prisoner, in jail in Kinshasa, under circumstances that have drawn condemnation from Amnesty International and the Red Cross. The government there has issued no word on when, or if, he will be released.

At the Ziatys' home, the arrest has a similarly jarring effect. Jeremiah locks himself in his room and cries himself to sleep.

BATTLING TO THE END

It's late October, and with just two weeks left in the season, a minor miracle occurs in the arrival of two 10-foot-long cardboard boxes: portable soccer goals for the Fugees. The administrator at the Y.M.C.A. finally put in the order. Ms. Mufleh and Ms. Ediger assemble the goals in Milam Park.

The goals and the new field offer Ms. Mufleh new opportunities to coach. On grass, players can slide-tackle during scrimmages, a danger on the old, gravelly field. A lined field makes it easier to practice throw-ins and corner kicks. And goals: well, they provide a chance for the Fugees to practice shooting.

A disturbing trend has emerged in recent games. The Fugees move the ball down the field at will, but their shots are wild. They tie two games despite dominating play.

Perhaps the Fugees are missing shots for the reason other teams miss shots: because scoring in soccer, under the best conditions, is deceptively difficult. But Ms. Mufleh also wonders if the absence of goals for most of a season doesn't have something to do with it.

Even so, the Fugees end the regular season on a misty Saturday with a 2–1 victory, to finish third in their division with a record of 5–2–3, behind undefeated Athens and the Dacula Danger, a team the Fugees tied. The season finale will be a tournament called the Tornado Cup. To a player, the Fugees think they can win.

"What makes us work as a team is we all want to win bad—we want to be the best team around," Qendrim says. "It's like they're all from my own country," he adds of his teammates. "They're my brothers."

* * * * * * *

The Tornado Cup comes down to a game between the Fugees and the Concorde Fire, perhaps Atlanta's most elite—and expensive—soccer academy. The Fugees need to win to advance to the finals.

Standing on the sideline in a sweatshirt with "Soccer Mom" on the back, Nancy Daffner, team mother for the Fire, describes her son's teammates as "overachievers." One is a cellist who has played with the Atlanta Symphony. Her son wakes up an hour early every day to do a morning radio broadcast at his school.

The Fire are mostly from the well-to-do Atlanta suburb of Alpharetta. They have played together under the same coach for five years. They practice twice a week under lights, and have sessions for speed and agility training.

Over the years, the parents have grown close. During practice, Ms. Daffner says, she and the other mothers often meet for margaritas while the fathers watch their sons play. The team has pool parties and players spend weekends at one another's lake houses. In the summer, most of the players attend soccer camp at Clemson University. Ms. Daffner estimates that the cost of playing for the Fire exceeds $5,000 a year per player, which includes fees, travel to tournaments and, of course, gear. Each player has an Adidas soccer bag embroidered with his jersey number.

There is one other expenditure. The parents of the Fire collectively finance the play of Jorge Pinzon, a Colombian immigrant and the son of a single working mother. He isn't from Alpharetta, but from East Gwinnett County, a largely Latino area outside Atlanta. Fire parents go to great lengths to get Jorge to games, arranging to meet him at gas stations around his home, landmarks they can find in his out-of-the-way neighborhood. Jorge is the best player on the team.

Ms. Mufleh gathers the Fugees before warm-ups.

"Play to the whistle," she tells them. "If the ref makes a bad call, you keep playing. O.K.? You focus on the game and how you're going to win it. Because if you don't, we're going to lose your last game of the season, and you're going home early."

Just before the opening whistle, some of the Fugees see a strange sight on the sideline. A teacher from the school of Josiah Saydee, a Liberian forward, has come to see him play. Some older refugee children from the complexes in Clarkston have managed rides to the game, an hour from home. Several volunteers from resettlement agencies show up. For the first time all year, the Fugees have fans.

The Fugees come out shooting—and missing—frequently. They lead, 1–0, at the half. In the second half, it's as if a force field protects the Fire's goal. After a half-dozen misses, the Fugees score again midway through the second half, to lead by 2–1.

Then, with just minutes to go, Jorge Pinzon of the Fire gets free about 25 yards from the Fugees' goal. He squares his shoulders and leans into a shot that arcs beautifully over the players' heads. Eldin Subasic, the Fugees' Bosnian goalie, leaps. The ball brushes his hands and deflects just under the bar, tying the game.

The final whistle blows moments later. The Fugees' season is over.

"You had them," Ms. Mufleh tells her team after the game. "You had them at 2 to 1, and you wouldn't finish it."

The Fugees are crushed.

"We lost, I mean, we tied our game," says Mafoday Jawneh, the sensitive newcomer to the team. "It was so. . . . " His voice trails off. "I don't know what it was."

AN UNPLEASANT HOLIDAY GIFT

The holidays are a festive time in Clarkston. Santa Claus arrives by helicopter at City Hall. The mayor is there to greet him, as are some of the Fugees.

They have other concerns besides Christmas. The Fugees have held two carwashes in town, to raise $1,000 to go to a tournament in Savannah in late January. They have come up $130 short, and Ms. Mufleh tells them that unless they raise the money, they are not going. When one player suggests asking their parents, Ms. Mufleh says that any player who asks a parent for tournament money will be kicked off the team.

She tells them, "You need to ask yourselves what you need to do for your team."

* * * * * * *

"You need to ask yourself what you need to do for your team," Jeremiah Ziaty says.

He is at home in his kitchen, talking with Prince Tarlue, a teammate from Liberia, making a case for a team project. Some of the boys are to meet at Eldin Subasic's apartment. They can knock on doors in town and offer to rake leaves to raise the money to get to Savannah. No need telling Coach, unless they raise enough cash. Prince says he is in. Grace is in, too. Some older boys in the refugee community offer to help out as well. Late on a Sunday morning, they set out.

That afternoon, Ms. Mufleh's cellphone rings. It's Eldin, who asks if she will pick up Grace and take him home. They have been raking leaves all day, he says, and Grace does not want to walk home in the dark. Oh, Eldin adds, he wants to give her the money.

"What money?" she asks.

"You said we needed $130," he tells her. "So we got $130."

* * * * * * *

Ms. Mufleh and Ms. Ediger, the team manager, spend the holiday vacation visiting the players' families. On Dec. 26, Ms. Mufleh receives a fax on Town of Clarkston letterhead.

Effectively immediately, the fax informs her, the Fugees soccer team is no longer welcome to play at Milam Park. The city is handing the field to a youth sports coordinator who plans to run a youth baseball and football program.

Questioned by this reporter, Mayor Swaney says he has forgotten that in October the City Council gave the Fugees six months. A few days later, he tells Ms. Mufleh the team can stay through March.

In early January, Ms. Mufleh logs on to Google Earth, and scans satellite images of Clarkston. There are green patches on the campuses of Georgia Perimeter College, and at the Atlanta Area School for the Deaf, around the corner from City Hall. She hopes to find the Fugees a permanent home.

CORRECTION: FEBRUARY 1, 2007

A front-page article on Jan. 21 about a soccer program for refugee boys in Clarkston, Ga., rendered incorrectly a quotation from The Atlanta Journal-Constitution in which Mayor Lee Swaney of Clarkston commented on the use of a town park. He said, "There will be nothing but baseball down there as long as I am mayor." He did not say "baseball and football."

EDITORS' NOTE: MARCH 4, 2007

A front-page article on Jan. 21 reported on a soccer program for refugee boys in Clarkston, Ga., and how it has come to symbolize the passions that run high in the area over the issue of immigration. The article included a statement that Clarkston's mayor, Lee Swaney, had forced the resignation of the town's longtime police chief, in part because of complaints from refugees that police officers were harassing them.

The former police chief, Charles Nelson—who was not identified by name in the article—called The Times on Feb. 5 to say that he had resigned voluntarily. Mayor Swaney says that Mr. Nelson left on his own accord.

The Times tried several times to contact Mr. Nelson for comment before publication. The article should have said that he could not be reached, and it should have attributed the information about the circumstances of his resignation to those who provided it.

APPENDIX VI

Legislation Introduced in the Georgia General Assembly, April 2003

HOUSE BILL 1002

By: Representatives Drenner of the 57th, Mobley of the 58th, Marin of the 66th, and Benfield of the 56th, Post 1

A BILL TO BE ENTITLED

AN ACT To amend Chapter 60 of Title 36 of the Official Code of Georgia Annotated, relating to general provisions applicable to counties and municipalities, so as to provide that voluntary agencies that assist with the resettlement of refugees must make certain reports to the county and municipality in which such agencies are located; to provide a definition; to repeal conflicting laws; and for other purposes.

Be it enacted by the General Assembly of Georgia:

Section 1. Chapter 60 of Title 36 of the Official Code of Georgia Annotated, relating to general provisions applicable to counties and municipalities, is amended by adding a new Code Section 36‑60‑24 to read as follows:

"36‑60‑24.

"Any voluntary agency that is involved in the resettlement of refugees in this state shall report to the governing authority of the county and, if located within a municipality, to the governing authority of the municipality in which such agency is located each time that such agency resettles or assists in the resettlement of ten or more refugees at one time in such county or municipality within ten days of such refugees arrival in the county. For the purposes of this Code section, 'voluntary agency' shall mean an agency located in this state that contracts with the United States Department of State or a National Voluntary Resettlement Agency to provide reception and placement services to refugees who reside in this state."

Section 2. All laws and parts of laws in conflict with this Act are repealed.

APPENDIX VII

Acronyms

FY—Fiscal Year
PRM—Bureau of Population, Refugees and Migration
ESL— English as Second Language
USRAP—U.S. Refugee Admissions Program
GAO—Government Accountability Office
ORR—Office of Refugee Resettlement
MARTA—Metropolitan Atlanta Rapid Transit Authority

○

CPSIA information can be obtained
at www.ICGtesting.com
Printed in the USA
LVHW060952290522
720026LV00012B/352